CW00407176

WITHDRAWN

THE MAKING OF THE UNITED KINGD

13593

The Making of the United Kingdom 1500-1750

Social Change

Peter Hepplewhite and Neil Tonge

WAYLAND

The Making of the United Kingdom 1500-1750

Church and People
Crown and Parliament
Social Change
Unification

Cover: *Covent Garden with St Paul's Church*, painted about 1750. This painting is in the Guildhall Art Gallery, Corporation of London: (inset) a May Day fair.

Series and Book Editor: Rosemary Ashley
Designer: Joyce Chester

First published in 1996 by Wayland (Publishers) Limited, 61 Western Road, Hove, East Sussex, BN3 1JD, England

British Library Cataloguing in Publication Data
Hepplewhite, Peter
 Social change. – (The making of the United Kingdom, 1500–1750)
 1.Great Britain – Social conditions – Juvenile literature 2.Great Britain – History – Tudors, 1485–1603 – Juvenile literature 3.Great Britain – History – Stuarts, 1603–1714 – Juvenile literature
 I.Title II.Tonge, Neil
 941'.05

ISBN 0-7502-1814-2

Typeset by Joyce Chester
Printed and bound in Italy by G. Canale & C.S.p.A., Turin

Picture acknowledgements
The pictures in this book were supplied by Bridgeman Art Library/Victoria and Albert Museum 8, /Cheltenham Art Gallery and Museums 14, /City of Bristol Museums and Art Gallery 17, /Tichborne Park 23, /Collection of the Earl of Derby 26, /Hatfield House 28, /Weston Park Foundation 36, /British Library 39, /New York Public Library 40; Mary Evans Picture Library 10, 16, 20, 22 (top), 24, 29, 30, 31, 32, 37 (both), 44; National Maritime Museum 7; Ann Ronan at Image Select 5, 11, 18, 19, 22; Philip Sauvain 15; Wayland Picture Library 9, 12, 21, 25, 27, /National Portrait Gallery 33, 34 (top), /Tate Gallery 34 (lower), 35, 36, 40. Artwork on pages 4, 13, 38, 42, 43 is by Peter Bull Design.

Contents

1

A Visitor to Britain in 1500

Imagine it is the year 1500 and you have been sent as a foreign ambassador to Britain. What would you find when you stepped ashore? Probably the first thing that would strike you would be the absence of people. Fewer than five million people lived in Britain in those days, compared to fifty-four million today. Most people lived in the south of England, south of the Rivers Humber and Severn.

A map showing the population and main industries of the British Isles in 1500.

Ireland. The largest town, Dublin, and surrounding area was controlled by the English, who planned to conquer the rest of the country. Most people were poor farmers, loyal to their clan chieftains.

Scotland, capital Edinburgh. There was little farming because of infertile land. Main exports were linen, coal and salt. The population was divided between English-speaking lowland Scots and Gaelic-speaking highlanders.

England, capital London. Much of the fertile country-side was farmed. Main exports were wool and woollen cloth, and there were small iron, coal and salt industries. Most of the population lived in the south.

SCOTLAND (750,000)

Aberdeen (3,000)

Dundee (3,000)

Perth (3,000)

Edinburgh (20,000)

Newcastle (10,000)

IRELAND (1,500,000)

York (10,000)

Galway (4,000)

Dublin (5,000)

Limerick (3,000)

WALES (280,000)

ENGLAND (2,750,000)

Norwich (12,700)

Waterford (2,400)

Cork (2,400)

Swansea (1,000)

London (60,000)

Cardiff (1,000)

Bristol (10,000)

Exeter (8,000)

Wales, capital Cardiff. The infertile land supported little farming. Wales had been conquered by the English in 1282 and was officially united with England in 1536.

In 1497 the Venetian ambassador, Andreas Franciscus, arrived in Britain from Italy and travelled on horseback throughout England. This is an extract from a letter that he wrote:

These people are great lovers of themselves and think they do anything better than other countries. They keep an enormous number of sheep which give them best quality wool. London is the capital and stands on the banks of the Thames. It has every luxury you can imagine but the streets are so badly paved that there is a huge amount of evil-smelling mud which lasts nearly all year round.

At the head of Scotland is a king who rules very fierce and brave tribes who are always the enemies of the English and often at war with them.

As regards Ireland, their life is poor and the clothing rough and greasy. But I would be wrong to put in writing things I had not seen myself, so I will leave it to people who can travel farther.

During the 1720s Daniel Defoe, author of *Robinson Crusoe*, made extensive journeys throughout Britain. In his introduction to *A Tour through the whole Island of Great Britain*, written between 1724–6, he wrote:

The preparation for this work has included seventeen large circuits and three tours over almost the whole English part of the island. I owe little debt to other men's labours and very few accounts other than that which I have been an eyewitness myself. It must be acknowledged that some foreigners, who have pretended to travel into England, and to give account of things when they come home, have treated us in a very indifferent manner: they have viewed us with envy.

Further north the population was sparse, scattered through the Scottish highlands, the Welsh uplands and the rolling plains and hills of Ireland. In 1500 the landscape was mainly woodland and heath, studded here and there with clusters of houses and farms. There were few towns, most of them little larger than villages are today.

On the seas around Britain you would see ships with billowing sails, many carrying wool and woollen cloth to the Low Countries (Holland and Belgium). Wool was England's richest trade, and English woollen goods were famous throughout Europe. You would also see ships carrying coal from Newcastle to London, and brigs laden with salt from Cheshire, tin from Cornwall and lead from Hull. Some ships would be heading towards Britain from other countries, bringing timber, fish and furs from the Baltic; wine, olive oil, leather, wax and fruit from France and Spain, and silks, spices and dyes from the Far East. Only a few years earlier

Naval ships belonging to the fleet built by Henry VIII to defend England. The daring exploits of English seamen, especially during the reign of Elizabeth I, led, eventually, to Britain acquiring a vast overseas empire.

Spanish explorers had ventured across the Atlantic Ocean, first landing in the Americas in 1492. But in 1500, Britain lagged behind the rush to explore the 'New World' and it would be eighty years before the first British colonies were established there.

At this time England was ruled by a Tudor king. After a long period of civil war, known as the Wars of the Roses, Henry VII had come to power following the bloody battle at Market Bosworth in 1485. North of the border with Scotland, Stuart kings attempted to keep order in their unruly realm. There were frequent raids and skirmishes between the two kingdoms. Wales, however, had long since been conquered by English kings, but the country remained proud of its own separate identity. Across the Irish sea the English monarchs had kept a toehold around Dublin, but in other parts of the island the land was divided among chieftains, who quarrelled and fought between themselves.

If you looked closer at English society, you would find that it too was divided. At the top of the social scale were the nobility – dukes, marquises, earls and barons, who had all been given their titles by the king, or, as eldest sons, had inherited them from their fathers. Next in importance were the knights and gentry. Below them were the citizens or burgesses who governed the towns, and the yeomen or peasant farmers. Finally, the fourth social class consisted of craftsmen and a step below them, farm labourers.

Leaping forward two hundred and fifty years, to 1750, what would the descendant of the ambassador see now? Despite terrible set-backs he would see that the population had climbed steadily to eight million. Although agriculture still dominated society and the economy, the pattern of agricultural land was now beginning to change. During Elizabeth's reign (1558–1603), more land had been given over to sheep, to feed the huge demand for English wool on the continent of Europe. By the 1750s the vast open fields were beginning to disappear, to be replaced by a patchwork of fields enclosed by hedges and fences.

By this time England, eager to take over her neighbours, had become part of a United Kingdom. Wales, already conquered, had been governed directly by England since 1536. In 1603, Scotland's Stuart king, James VI, also became King James I of England.

In Ireland, Queen Elizabeth's armies had defeated the mainly Roman Catholic people, who were treated as a conquered race. Laws were passed against the Irish Catholics which prevented them from obtaining important positions. Even their land was snatched away from them. Meanwhile, as England's power grew, so too did the nation's wealth. Although England was late in developing overseas trade and establishing colonies in newly explored lands,

Colonists in the seventeenth century preparing to set sail on the long and dangerous voyage across the Atlantic Ocean, to settlements in North America.

The development of overseas trade changed many of the social habits of the British. Tea drinking became very popular, but only among the rich at first, because of its high price. This picture shows a wealthy family drinking Indian tea in the eighteenth century.

by 1750 the country had become a leading world power. Trading connections led to the building of forts overseas to protect trade routes. These forts had led to the conquest of surrounding lands, and were to be the seeds of an empire which would flower a hundred years later.

Trade, in turn, led to changes in society and the economy of Britain. A powerful class of merchants had risen, owing its strength to trade. These merchants had bought estates and joined the nobility, or had married their sons and daughters into older, powerful families. Wool and woollen cloth was still the most important trade. Centres of industry were located in East Anglia, Yorkshire and the south west of England and towns had grown in size and importance. Many other regions were beginning to specialize, concentrating on making or growing particular products.

In 1750 Britain was poised to become the most powerful country in the world. This achievement had been built upon the power of trade which, in turn, was to change Britain into the world's first industrial nation.

How did this transformation take place? How did Britain, in 1500 a small disunited island, rise to become, in 1750, a leading world power? This book will trace and explain these changes to you, the time traveller.

2

Rural Life

When Henry VIII became king in 1509, as many as nine out of ten people lived in the countryside. When George II died in 1760, the figure was still high, as many as eight out of ten. Over this two-hundred-and-fifty-year period the landscape was transformed by

Who were the people in early modern England?

The government first took a census (count) of the population in 1801. For the years before this historians can only estimate the numbers. One of their main sources of evidence for these earlier years are parish registers. In 1538, Thomas Cromwell, Henry VIII's chancellor, ordered each parish to keep a record of its births, marriages and deaths. This example comes from Countesthorpe in Leicestershire.

The Christenings Burials and Weddings in our towne from the 25th of March 1646 unto the 25th of March 1647.
Robert the sonne of Thomas Wyers husbandman was baptized the 25th of March.
And he was buried the same day.
Grace Jacksonn Widdow was buried the 27th of March.
John the sonne of Simon Smeeton was baptized the 3rd of March.
Thomas the sonne of Richard Bent blacksmyth and Anne his wife was baptized the 24th of March.
Elizabeth Bent widd. was buried the 28th of May.
Anne the wife of Richard Bent blacksmyth was buried the 9th of June.
Elizabeth Freer the daughter of Willm. Freer miller & Frances his wife was baptized the 6th of September.

Life in the countryside meant grindingly hard work for most people. The man in the foreground is cutting wood for fuel. In the background, farmworkers can be seen ploughing, cutting corn and sowing seeds.

improvements in farming. The driving force behind these improvements was a rapidly growing population. In England this rose from about 2.6 million in 1500 to approximately 5.7 million in 1750. The great achievement of the age was producing enough food to meet the needs of all these people.

In 1500 the countryside was farmed much as it had been in the Middle Ages. The three-field system was common, especially in the Midlands. Villagers farming in this way rented strips of land from the Lord of the Manor. These strips were scattered across huge fields. Every third year one field was left to lie fallow, without crops, to recover its fertility. In other areas, such as Kent or Devon, land was divided by hedges or walls in a patchwork of small fields. In many areas farmers had the right to keep animals and collect fuel in local wastelands, woodlands and commons.

The way people behaved towards each other depended on the rank or social class they were born into. This was described by a country priest, William Harrison, in 1577:

We in England divide our people into four sorts, gentlemen, citizens or burgesses, yeomen and labourers.

Saving every penny was important. This woman is using a spinning wheel to spin wool into thread. She would then weave the thread into cloth and either sell it to a merchant or make clothes for her family. A noble can be seen hunting with his servant and dogs in the background.

How to become a noble

1. Inherit your title from your father
2. Earn it for services to the monarch, for example fighting in a war
3. Buy it! Hard up kings and queens sold titles for cash

Noblemen with an armed attendant during the reign of Elizabeth I. Their elegant clothes show that they were wealthy men.

Three of Harrison's 'sorts' were found in the country. The top rank were the 'gentlemen', or nobles. Although they made up only about two per cent of the population they owned well over half the country. Their incomes came from renting out land. Some were extremely wealthy, as was shown by their lifestyles. They built grand new houses, elegantly decorated and furnished.

Gentlemen expected their tenants to respect them. John Bankes was a landlord in Lancashire around 1600. He advised his son, 'never make a lease (an agreement to rent land) above one and twenty years, for so shall you keep your tenants in good and dutiful obedience to you.'

Beneath this top rank Harrison placed yeomen. He wrote that they had a 'certain pre-eminence' (social standing). They were able to 'live wealthy, keep good houses and travel to get riches'. Yeomen usually owned or rented large farms of at least fifty acres. Rich yeomen could expect to progress up the ladder to the rank of gentleman or nobility.

At the bottom were the 'fourth and last sort of people … day labourers, poor husbandmen, artificers and servants', who had 'neither voice nor authority in the common wealth (government), but are to be ruled and not to rule others.'

This fourth category included most of the population. Husbandmen ran small farms, sometimes only a few acres in size. Labourers worked for others but often had a small patch of land on which to grow vegetables. In times of good harvest both these groups could live well. In bad times they might be on the edge of starvation.

The rise in population meant that there was increased demand and high prices for farm produce. This encouraged those with most land to be better farmers – and make more money. In early Tudor times wool was a good cash crop.

A fifteenth-century wood-cut showing farmworkers hay-making.

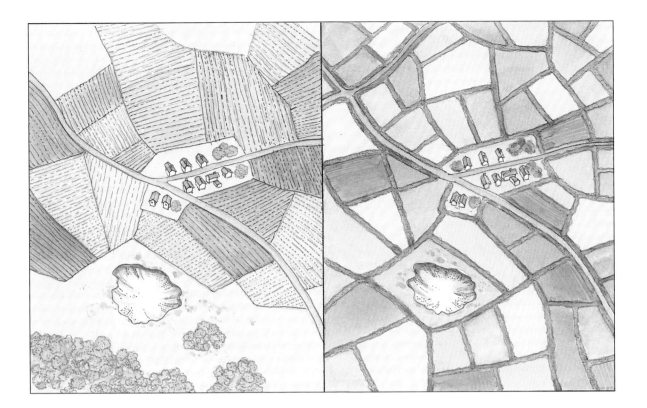

Between 1540 and 1546 the price of a tod (12.7 kg) of wool jumped from 6s 8d (34p) to £1.8d (£1.04p). Families such as the Spencers of Northamptonshire turned their land over to grazing. They made their fortune with vast flocks of over 30,000 sheep.

Some farmers began to specialize, perhaps to cater for the needs of nearby towns. Hops were grown in Suffolk and Kent, cider apples in Devon, and butter and cheese in the Vale of Glamorgan. In the early 1600s Sir Thomas Pelham, a Sussex gentleman, bought cattle from Cheshire and fattened them up for London butchers. Robert Loder, a Berkshire yeoman, grew 2,000 lb (907 kg) of cherries in 1617. He sent his maid to sell them at the local markets and made £12 – twice as much as a labourer had to live on all year.

The most important agricultural developments came with the introduction, around 1650, of new grasses such as clover and sainfoin (a crop used for animal fodder). These could feed more animals which in turn produced more dung. The dung was used as fertilizer and enriched the soil for important crops such as wheat and barley. It was no longer necessary to leave land fallow.

Smaller enclosed fields (right) gradually replaced the larger open fields of medieval times. Farming became more efficient but the poorer workers often lost the use of commons, woods and wastelands.

This painting shows the countryside around Dixton Manor House in Gloucestershire in the seventeenth century. The varied landscape of small hedged fields has been lost to us today because of a return to larger fields, due to mechanised farming methods.

Landowners realized that improvements worked best on land that was divided into separate fields. Sometimes these were sown from new land that had been hacked from forests or drained from marshes. But more usually the old open fields, commons and woods were fenced off or hedges were grown around them. This was known as enclosure. Often enclosure happened with the agreement of the villagers, but sometimes the landlord enclosed the fields against the wishes of the local people, using an Act of Parliament.

Overall, enclosure led to increased food production and bigger profits for the wealthier farmers. But life became even harder for poorer families. Rising prices also led to higher rents. In years of bad harvests, farmers could not grow enough crops to sell and pay their debts. Labourers found that they could buy less and less with their wages.

In the past, the labourers' traditional rights, such as keeping animals on the commons, helped them to survive. After enclosure, however, some were driven from the land while others became farm workers, relying on the goodwill of their employers. This led to angry protests. In Elizabethan England gangs of landless vagrants terrorised the countryside. Some enclosures led to long court cases while other poor villagers rioted and ripped out the new hedges and tore down the fences. They were trying in vain to restore a lost world.

3

Town Life

The second 'sort' of people described by William Harrison in 1577 (see page 10) were citizens and burgesses. These were the townspeople with enough wealth to run the affairs of the town. They also included professional people such as priests and lawyers. The fourth 'sort' that Harrison described (the labourers and craftsmen) lived in towns too. The wealthy often needed the services of all sorts of craftspeople, such as tailors and shoemakers, and the best place for these people to sell their services was in towns.

In 1500 most towns were very small, often only a handful of streets. Liverpool, Manchester and Birmingham were no more than large villages. Only London resembled what we would call a city, with a huge population of 60,000. Next in size were Norwich, with 10,000, York, 10,000, and Newcastle with 6,000. By 1750, however, one in five of the population lived in a town, and one hundred years after this about half of the population were townspeople.

This map, made in 1591, shows the River Thames flowing through a London which was at that time close to green fields. Even so, London was ten times the size of its nearest rivals, Bristol and Norwich, and was by far the most important town in England.

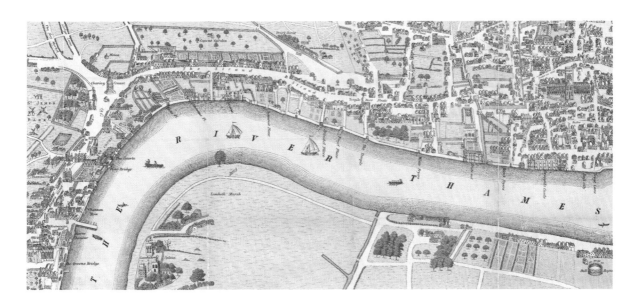

Why did this massive change come about? One of the most important reasons was trade. In the country, people could grow food and make their own clothes, but if they could make a little more to sell, they could buy extra goods for themselves. There had to be a suitable place where people could meet to buy and sell goods. Some built their houses at important crossroads, or near a bridge or ford, or in a sheltered cove where ships could anchor. Others chose to build their houses near a castle for protection, or near a monastery where travellers would come on pilgrimage. These groups of houses became the first towns, and as time passed, these towns became market places for the surrounding district.

The smell of these towns might well be overpowering. Streets were alleyways filled with mud and filth, with household rubbish and the contents of chamber pots thrown into them. Butchers and fishmongers would cut up produce outside their homes and throw the waste into the gutter running along the centre of the street. Streets were so narrow that wagons often got wedged. Upstairs rooms overhung the streets so far that it was possible to touch the

The old bridge leading into the city of Newcastle-upon-Tyne. At the beginning of the sixteenth century towns were protected from enemy soldiers and robbers by high walls. By the mid-eighteenth century, most towns had grown beyond their walls, which were often removed to allow for expansion.

building on the opposite side. Little wonder that terrible diseases, like plague, found a breeding ground and fires swept unchallenged through towns.

While the wealthy burgesses ran the towns, the craftsmen ran their own trades. All craftsmen had to belong to a guild. The first rung of the ladder of the guild system was occupied by the apprentices. An apprentice had to learn his trade for seven years and produce a 'masterpiece', before he could become a craftsman. He would then work for the master before becoming a master himself.

By 1750 towns had grown both in size and number. Newer towns were beginning to replace some of the Tudor towns. Bristol had grown in the seventeenth and early eighteenth centuries to become the second largest city in England after London. Other, newer towns were emerging: Liverpool (35,000), Manchester (45,000), Birmingham (30,000) and Leeds (14,000).

Bristol docks and quay in the early eighteenth century. By this time Bristol had grown to be the second largest city in the kingdom. Later, as trade with the Americas expanded, the port declined in importance.

17

Cutting and sewing clothes in a tailor's shop. All craftsmen in a town belonged to a guild which helped members and preserved the quality of the particular trade. Masters would employ journeymen to sell the products, and often the whole family would be involved in making the goods.

The reason for the rise of importance and size of these towns may be found by examining the contents of James Leach's shop in Bury. In 1668 he sold:

> *Textiles, thimbles, pins, hooks and eyes, needles and threads, lace, tape and ribbon, knitted stockings for men, women and children, tea from India, sugar from the West Indies, tobacco from the Americas.*

And so the list goes on.

Two things strike us from this list of goods. Firstly, some of the goods come from overseas. Between 1500 and 1750, British explorers had sought out suitable countries with which to build up trading links. Coffee, tea and sugar were all popular luxuries in the late seventeenth century. Many of these goods were expensive. Tobacco from the Americas, for example, cost £1 – £2 per lb (0.45 kg) in 1620. By 1700 so much was imported that the price had fallen to only one shilling (5p) per lb. Towns grew because trade grew, and much of this was new trade from overseas, particularly from the Americas.

Secondly, many of the goods in James Leach's shop were manufactured goods. Because of the rise in population in the sixteenth and early seventeenth centuries more and

Population of England

1500 2.6 million

1600 4.1 million

1650 5.2 million

1700 5 million

1750 5.7 million

more people, especially the cottagers, added to their earnings by manufacturing goods in their own homes. The merchant would bring the materials to their homes and return later to collect the finished articles. Lace, chains and nails were all made in this way. The increase in population also meant that there were more people wanting to buy manufactured goods. In some instances, large workshops would make goods that could not be made in peoples' homes, such as glass windows for the homes of the rich, or large iron goods such as those made by the Derby family at Coalbrookdale in the Midlands.

Because of these changes in the way goods were made, the guild system began to break down. Society became separated into the people who owned businesses and the workers who earned wages.

In the eighteenth century cottagers began renting machinery from masters, such as these weaving frames. The cloth was collected and sold at the cloth hall. This was called the domestic system, because goods were made in the home. It began to replace the guild system, because little skill was needed to operate such machines.

With no sanitation, clean drinking water or rubbish removal, streets became choked with filth and towns were a breeding ground for plague and other diseases.

Towns may have grown in size but they were still unhealthy places in which to live. Newer building materials such as bricks and tiles had made homes more comfortable, but there was still no sanitation. Drinking water was drawn from the nearest river or stream, where rubbish was frequently thrown. Toilets were open cesspits which could often overflow. One scourge, however, had disappeared. The plague made its last appearance in Britain at the end of the seventeenth century. Other diseases connected to poverty remained, including typhus and dysentery.

4

The Problem of Poverty

In 1558–9 the parish of St Peter Mancroft in Norwich spent £110 4s 4d (22p) on the care of the poor. Cases included:

> Item: *payd for ye nursing of a yong childe left in the parish 1s 8d* (8p)
>
> Item: *payd to ye cunstables for sending away of vagabonds* (beggars) *4s 8d* (23p)
>
> Item: *payed for ye keping of a poisened man in the tyme of his sickness £1. 13s 8d* (68p)

These records show the problems of looking after the poor. The costs were very great, and only a wealthy community would be able to raise more than £100. Some people

This scene in Elizabethan England shows a nobleman passing a beggar on a country road.

Beggars were a common sight in sixteenth century England.

(Below) This seventeenth-century print shows wealthy people fleeing from a town where plague has struck, leaving no work for the servants and labourers left behind.

grumbled but were prepared to pay to help those who clearly deserved it, such as the young and helpless or the sick. The fit and healthy were another matter. They were blamed for their own poverty and often treated harshly.

Poverty was nothing new. In the Middle Ages every town and village had its poor, but charity from the local church or wealthy landowner had usually provided enough for them to be looked after. During Tudor and Stuart times, however, the numbers of poor soared to between a quarter and a third of the population. In a year of bad harvests, about half the people needed help to survive.

The causes of poverty were many. The changes in town and countryside led to a huge number of workers earning barely enough money to support their families. Between 1500 and 1650 prices shot up faster than wages. Many were forced to move and look for work. But leaving their villages did not always help. The growing population meant that too many people were chasing too few jobs. Families tightened their belts but had little left for emergencies – and there were plenty of these.

The plague returned year after year between the Black Death of 1348, which claimed over a third of the population, and the Great Plague of 1666. Communities were sometimes devastated, for example, 6,000 people died in Norwich in 1579. When plague struck, trade was badly effected. Rich employers fled into the countryside and paid off their workers, while farmers were too frightened to take their goods to market in an infected town.

Poor weather and bad harvests were frequent. In 1648 Ralph Josselyn, an Essex vicar, wrote in his diary:

> *September 15, 1646. A marvellous wet season, winter coming early. Wheat this year was exceedingly smitten* (affected by the weather) *and dwindled and lank ... all manner of meats excessive dear, beef at cheapest, 2 1/2d* (1p) *per lb* (0.45 kg).
>
> *October 24, 1646. A wonderful sad wet season. ... much corn in many places ... rotted and spoiled in the fields; grass exceedingly trodden underfoot and spoiled by the cattle ... work very dead ... little corn sown ... fears of our utter ruin in the Kingdom.*

This picture is called The Tichborne Dole. It was painted in 1670 and shows the squire of the village of Tichborne in Hampshire giving out food to the poor. This event took place with great ceremony every year.

Conditions like these were a disaster for ordinary people. Often food shortages were followed by disease – in fact typhus, an illness which killed many people, was known as 'famine fever'.

Of all the poor, vagrants caused the most alarm. There had always been some travelling beggars but after 1500 their numbers shot up. In 1577 William Harrison (see page 10) estimated there were 10,000 vagrants. A century later, in 1695, Gregory King, who made a note of population figures,

Beggars and vagrants were punished by being tied to a cart and whipped around the town.

reckoned that there were 30,000. Many of these vagrants were simply looking for work and settled down if they found a job. But however unfair it seems to us, it was taken for granted that anyone 'on the road' was a rogue or a beggar.

There were some good reasons for this. Many people on the move caused trouble. The most feared were soldiers and sailors who had been disbanded after a war. They were often well armed and able to take what they wanted by force. In 1589 five hundred soldiers threatened to loot Bartholomew Fair in London and the city militia (defence force) had to be called out.

In 1568 Thomas Harman described a scary Elizabethan underworld in which gangs of beggars specialized in different ways of preying upon respectable people. These included:

Upright Men – leaders of gangs
Hookers – thieves who stole clothes from open windows
Palliards – beggars showing terrible scars or mutilations and demanding money
Priggers or *prancers* – horse thieves
Dommerers – people pretending to be deaf mutes.

The unrest and fear caused by vagrants pushed the government into taking action. Early laws ignored the difficulties of finding a job and tried to punish the healthy poor. In 1531, an Act of Parliament allowed vagrants to 'be tied to the end of a cart naked and be beaten with whips through the town'. In 1547, an even fiercer Act gave magistrates the power to brand beggars with a 'V' and make them slaves for two years.

A terrible harvest in 1597 led to rioting and hunger across the country. This finally convinced the government that some sort of relief arrangements had to be made. Between 1597 and 1601 a system for helping the poor was set up that lasted for the next two hundred years. This followed the example of cities like Norwich, where every parish had to appoint Overseers of the Poor to collect local rates (property taxes). These were to be used to give the unemployed work, pay for apprenticeships for poor children and provide the 'lame, impotent, old, blind and such' with items like clothes, food, fuel and rent.

The dancing skeleton of 'Death' snatches the life of a child. Four bad harvests in a row led to widespread famine and starvation in the north of England at the end of the sixteenth century. Although starvation was rare, malnutrition and disease were always present among the poor, leading to many early deaths.

5

Popular Culture

Richard Baxter, writing in 1664, recalled his childhood in a Shropshire village. His family were Puritans, a very strict branch of the Protestant religion, and they believed that Sundays should be spent in prayer and Bible study. Years later the memory of these Sundays still stung:

In the village where I lived the reader read the Common Prayer briefly and the rest of the day even till dark night ... was spent dancing under the May-pole and a great tree not far from my

A painting showing a group of men playing a game of cards during the Tudor period.

*father's door ... We could not read the Scripture ...
without the great disturbance of the tabor* (small
drum) *... and pipe and noise in the street. Many
times my mind was inclined among them.*

Nevertheless, Richard's description gives us rare evidence about a hidden past. Many customs and games were passed on only by word of mouth. The details are lost to us now and often the small amount of written information available is unfairly biased. Puritans, and for different, perhaps snobbish, reasons, gentlemen, often recorded the worst behaviour of the 'common people', such as their superstitions and heavy drinking.

The changing of the seasons was of vital importance at a time when everyone depended upon good harvests. The passing of the year was marked by customs so old that no one could remember how they began. In a few places these ancient ways still continue.

May Day was the time when people celebrated the arrival of summer, warmth and short nights. Everyone loved to dance around the maypole, especially the courting couples. The maypole represented a living tree and was a symbol of fertility. Today the maypole at Barwick in Elmet, near Leeds, proudly stands over twenty-three metres high.

Harvest meant the onset of autumn. The harvest supper was served to workers after the corn was gathered in. The last sheaf was saved and made into a corn dolly. This was believed to be where the female Corn Spirit hid. The dolly was kept in the farmhouse to make sure there was a good crop next year. Today, in some church harvest festivals, corn dollies are still given to the children.

Christmas marked the birth of Christ and the darkest time of year. The Christmas holidays lasted for twelve days. Mumming plays were performed in many villages. St George was the hero of these plays; he usually killed an enemy, frequently a Turkish swordsman. The dead man was often brought back to life by the Doctor.

Many communities held a parish festival to celebrate the saint for whom the local church was named. In different parts of the country this was known as the wake, revel or ale. All kinds of entertainments took place during a week of holiday. These might include a feast and drinking, singing, dancing, races, wrestling and football.

Music and dancing were an important part of this marriage feast at Bermondsey, which took place during the reign of Elizabeth I.

28

Football could be very rough. This is a description of the game as it was played in 1585.

A group of wealthy young men playing a rough and tumble game with a ball similar to a modern football. Players could strike the ball with hands and feet.

> *As for football playing, it may rather be called a friendly kind of fight. For doth not everyone lie in wait for his adversary (enemy) seeking to overthrow him and pitch him on his nose, though it be on hard stones or in a ditch, sometimes their necks are broken, sometimes their backs, sometimes their noses gush with blood.*

A similar traditional game is still played in Ashbourne in Derbyshire. There are no rules – and the goals are 4.5 km apart!

Other pastimes also seem rough or bloodthirsty compared to today. Cruelty to animals was common. Bulls or bears were baited – they were chained up and made to fight ferocious dogs. In cock-fights, cockerels with metal spurs around their legs pecked and gouged each other to death. Hunting deer and wild boar was a sport enjoyed by the rich. The poor would hunt hares and rabbits with specially trained dogs, but less for a pastime – more as a necessity, to feed hungry families.

A noisy crowd places bets at a cock fight. This scene and the bear baiting (opposite) took place in the eighteenth century.

Many people, too, were treated little better than the animals. Criminals were punished in public and crowds gathered while beggars were whipped or thieves put in the stocks. The greatest show was a public execution. Usually this was a simple hanging, but sometimes a traitor might be 'hung, drawn and quartered'. In this savage death the poor prisoners were hanged first but let down while still alive. Next they were cut open at the stomach and their intestines pulled out. Finally they were beheaded and their bodies chopped into four pieces.

Watching drama was popular with rich and poor alike. Audiences expected spectacular performances with blood, severed heads, earthquakes, floods and fires. In religious plays Jesus Christ had to be seen to suffer on the cross and the Devil appeared in clouds of sulphurous smoke.

In 1576 the first two purpose-built playhouses were opened in London. By 1605 as many as one in seven of the capital's population visited the theatre every week. All new plays had to be approved by the Lord Chancellor, and during the reign of Elizabeth I especially, drama was often used as propaganda for political purposes, to persuade people that the government was right.

This helped the career of William Shakespeare (1564–1616), the greatest playwright of his time. The theatre company he wrote for performed with Queen Elizabeth's approval and became known as the Queen's Men. To keep on the good side of the Queen, Shakespeare's plays had to show the greatness of the Tudor family and England. This went down well with patriotic audiences.

In 1500 most people could not read and write. By 1750 more than half the population could read even if they could not write. The growing number of printing presses brought about what some historians have called an 'information revolution'. A new market opened up for cheap literature. Ordinary people bought ballads and chapbooks (short booklets) joke books and almanacs (books of astrology).

These men are watching the sport of bear baiting. Fighting dogs were specially bred to take part in what seems to us a very cruel sport.

31

*The Globe Theatre, near
the River Thames in
London, where people
went to watch the plays of
Shakespeare and other
writers.*

By far the best selling book was the Bible. The first Bible
to be published in English, rather than Latin, was approved
by Henry VIII in 1539. More famous was the Authorised
Version, published in 1611 with the blessing of King James I.
Only 8,000 different words were used. They were chosen to
read easily, especially out loud. The simple but poetic
language has influenced writers ever since.

Mystery plays

In towns, one of the duties of the guilds was the staging of
the miracle or mystery plays at Easter. When the Guild of
Masons was set up in Newcastle in 1581, their rules
included this duty:

> *During the Corpus Christi plays to play The
> Burial of Our Lady St Mary the Virgin. Any
> absent brother* (member) *to forfeit* (pay) *2s 6d*
> (12.5p).

6

A Woman's Lot

Queen Elizabeth I was one of England's greatest monarchs. She was admired for her cleverness and skill in dealing with other countries. Yet in spite of her marvellous example, almost everyone agreed that women were inferior to men. When William Harrison wrote about his four 'sorts' of people (see chapter 2) he did not include women. He took it for granted that they took their place in life from their fathers or husbands.

This portrait of Queen Elizabeth I was made soon after she came to the throne. Although Elizabeth was a very successful monarch, and she never married, most women were seen as the property of men during the sixteenth, seventeenth and eighteenth centuries.

Women in the fields worked as hard as the men, in the sixteenth century.

Poor education meant that it was hard for women to be independent. From 1536, parishes were ordered to give religious instruction and reading lessons to all children, but this teaching was very basic. Grammar schools (set up to teach Latin and Greek), and universities would not accept girls. For rich families there were a growing number of girls' day or boarding schools. However the subjects – the Bible, writing, needlework, dancing and music – were taught to help young ladies become charming wives.

This painting, known as The Cholmondeley Sisters, *shows two sisters who were born on the same day, married on the same day and had their babies on the same day. The painting is in London's Tate Gallery.*

Most people agreed with the ideas of King James I, when he refused to allow his daughter, Elizabeth, to learn Latin:

> *To make women learned and foxes tame has the same effect, to make them more cunning.*

It was assumed that the main aim in life for a woman was to be a good wife. In the 1500s many marriages were arranged by parents, who rarely asked the views of their children. By 1750 things had changed sharply. Young people chose their own partners, and usually parents gave their consent. This was the beginning of the family as we know it.

In Shakespeare's *Romeo and Juliet*, Juliet married at the age of fourteen. But this was not the case with most women. Teenage brides were rare. A study of 1,000 marriage licences in Canterbury between 1619 and 1660 shows the average age of brides was about twenty-four. Their husbands were usually three or four years older.

Family life varied according to how rich people were, but in all social classes the husband was expected to be in charge of the household. In 1622 an author, William Gouge, wrote a book of advice for newly-weds called *Of Domestical Duties.*

> *The husband is the highest in the family, and hath authority over all committed to his charge. He is as a king in his owne house.*

A husband beating his wife in the 1600s, while the children play beside her. The law did not prevent a husband beating his wife, although other family members might step in if he became too violent.

This sixteenth-century scene shows a wealthy woman in her bedchamber soon after she has given birth. We can see from the unhygienic conditions and all the 'goings-on' taking place in the room, that many mothers and new babies often ran high risks of infection.

However Gouge pointed out that a married man had duties to protect and care for his family and added:

> *If love be not the guiding hand in the husband there is like to be little peace between man and wife.*

A rich wife was valued for the land or money she brought with her. Once married, all of this belonged to her husband. It was not until the nineteenth century (during the reign of Queen Victoria) that married women gained the right to keep their own property.

In ordinary families a new wife would be important for the work she could do. Her hands would be full in the country, as Anthony Fitzherbert described in 1523 in his *Boke of Husbandrie* (Book of Farming).

> *It is a wive's occupation to winnow all manner of corn, to make malt, wash and wring, to make hay, shear corn, and in time of need to help her husband fill the muck wain (waggon), drive the plough, to load hay and such other ... to go to market to sell butter, cheese, milk, eggs, chickens, capons, hens, pigs, geese and all manner of corn.*

An engraving illustrating 'Death' taking the life of a young woman. It shows how even someone in the prime of life could be suddenly struck down at any time.

A dangerous time for women was when they gave birth. Midwives were poorly trained, and the unhygienic conditions meant that there was always a high risk of infection. In 1684 a typically sad incident was recorded:

> *Mistress Earnshaw of York was in sore labour, had her child pulled from her slowly, died at last, left a sad husband.*

Married women expected to spend several years of their adult lives being pregnant or 'great bellied'. They also expected many of their children to die. In 1650, Elizabeth Walker married a chemist in London. She gave birth to eleven children, eight of whom died as babies. The three survivors were all girls. However, little Mary died at six, Elizabeth at sixteen and the last daughter died giving birth to Johnny, Elizabeth's grandson.

During the Civil War (1642–49) society was in upheaval and women frequently showed how tough they could be. One famous woman, Lady Bankes, defended Corfe Castle, in Dorset, against two sieges by Parliamentary armies. After the war, the Duchess of Newcastle complained that

> *'too many women now behaved like men. ... the war had led them to Swagger, Game (gamble), to drink, to revell and to make factions (quarrel).'*

37

7

Trade and Commerce

A map showing Britain's trade with Europe in the sixteenth century.

From the late 1400s onwards, European seamen began to sail the uncharted waters of the oceans. They made these risky voyages in the hope of gaining their fortunes through trade, and the goods they sought more than any other were spices. Spices were valuable for flavouring and preserving food that had to be stored throughout the winter. Although the dangers of shipwreck or attack by unfriendly peoples were great, the risks were worth taking for the fortunes that could be made from this trade.

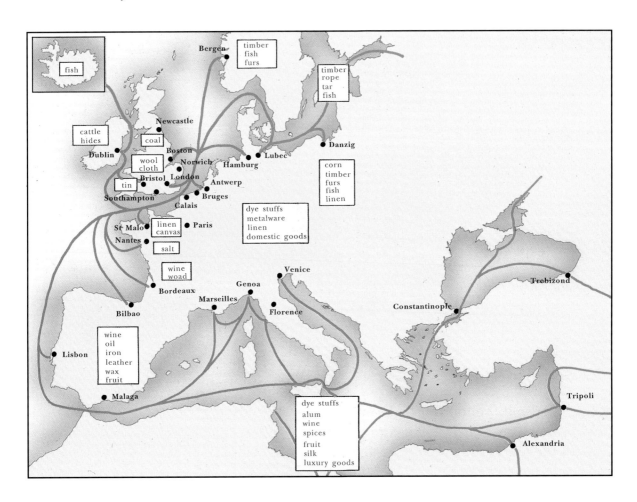

England was a latecomer to this race. In the late 1490s the voyages of John and Sebastian Cabot, who discovered rich fishing grounds off the coast of Newfoundland, were the only explorations that England could boast of. But it was the attraction of finding a route to the East and obtaining spices that continued to act as a magnet to English and European explorers. In 1553 Hugh Willoughby and Richard Chancellor tried to 'drive' their ship through the thick pack ice north of Russia in an attempt to discover a north-east passage to India. Willoughby died on the coast of Lapland (northern Russia) but Chancellor continued the journey overland to Moscow, where he set up a valuable trade in furs and timber. In a desperate search for an alternative route, English explorers attempted to find a 'north-west passage' around the top of North America. Henry Hudson, Martin Frobisher and John Davis all failed to find a way through the ice. In the process, however, they laid claim to large tracts of North America for Britain.

Many explorers tried unsuccessfully to find a 'passage', north-east around northern Russia, and north-west around northern Canada.

The Spanish colony of San Domingo under attack from Francis Drake. Spain had been the first European country to establish an empire in the Americas. Expeditions led by Elizabethan buccaneers attacked and robbed Spanish ships carrying gold and silver from South America back to Spain.

In other parts of the Americas, English seamen began as pirates, plundering the treasures carried by Spanish ships from South America back to Spain. In the 1560s John Hawkins tried to break into the flourishing slave trade between West Africa and Spanish America, but without much success. In reprisal for this lack of success, Francis Drake launched attacks on the Spanish possessions and returned to England via the western route around Africa. In this way he became the first Englishman to circumnavigate the world.

In North America Walter Raleigh and his half-brother, Humphrey Gilbert, attempted to set up colonies. Although these failed, they paved the way for permanent colonies in Virginia which later supplied the people of the British Isles with the new and growing habit of tobacco smoking.

The slave trade

In the early part of the sixteenth century convicts were shipped from Europe across the Atlantic to work in the cotton and tobacco plantations of North America. But they were not used to the climate and many died. Moreover there were never enough of them to work the plantations.

A solution to the problem was found by a merchant who landed in West Africa in 1518. He bought some prisoners from an African chieftain, shipped them across the Atlantic and sold them as slaves. Fortunes could be made from the sufferings of this human cargo and much of England's wealth came from this shameful trade. Over 9 million Africans were taken across to the Americas during the next 150 years, until the possession of slaves was finally abolished throughout the British Empire in 1833.

TO BE SOLD, on board the Ship *Bance-Island*, on tuefday the 6th of *May* next, at *Afhley-Ferry*; a choice cargo of about 250 fine healthy NEGROES, juft arrived from the Windward & Rice Coaft. —The utmoft care has already been taken, and fhall be continued, to keep them free from the leaft danger of being infected with the SMALL-POX, no boat having been on board, and all other communication with people from *Charles-Town* prevented. *Auftin, Laurens, & Appleby.*

A notice advertising slaves for sale.

By the mid-seventeenth century British trade had spread to many parts of the world, including North America and the West Indies, and the Far East. The British Government could not protect trade in all these distant places, so merchants formed themselves into trading companies and provided for their own defence. Each company was given a charter by the government which stated that the company could trade only in a particular part of the world.

The most famous of these trading companies was the East India Company. This company was formed in 1600, originally to take part in the spice trade in the East Indies. After being driven out of the islands by Dutch colonists, the company developed trade with India. The East India Company became fabulously wealthy, eventually ruling over most of India. In the nineteenth century, power was transferred from the company to the British government.

In the race for overseas trade Britain had to compete with Spain, France and Holland. The result was that Britain became involved in wars with all these countries. By the eighteenth century the nation emerged as the winner and the prize was a vast overseas empire. The colonies provided raw materials for British industry as well as a market for British manufactured goods.

Britain's internal trade grew at the same speed as her overseas trade. In the sixteenth century, England's economy was based on a network of country town markets serving their local region. Trade between the regions was on a very small scale and mostly carried on through travelling fairs which traded in special goods. Communications were poor.

Trading commodities and empires in 1750.

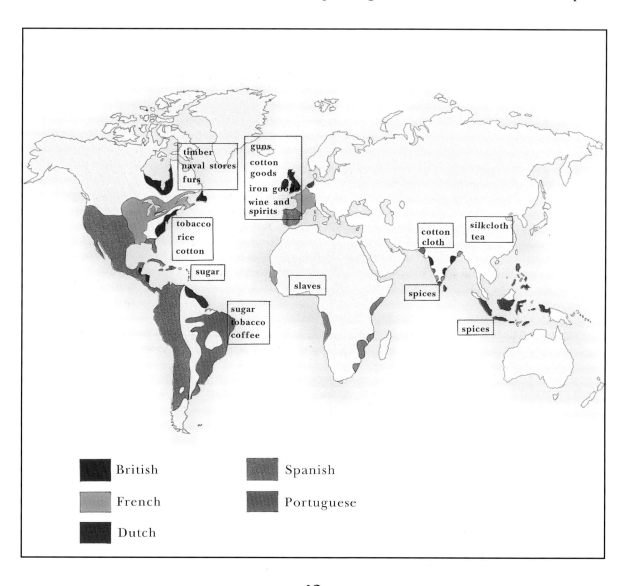

British	Spanish
French	Portuguese
Dutch	

hat *made from* felt *in* Leicester

shirt *made from* linen *in* Lancashire or Scotland

coat *made from* woollen cloth *in* Yorkshire

buttons *made from* metal *in* Birmingham

waistcoat *made from* calico *in* Norwich

buttons *made from* bone *in* Macclesfield

gloves *made from* leather *in* Somerset

coat lining *made from* shaloon (fine wool) *in* Berkshire

breeches *made from* drugget (wool and linen mixture) *in* Devizes

stockings *made from* woollen yarn *in* Westmoreland

No new roads had been constructed since the Roman occupation fifteen centuries earlier. Roads were little more than strips of deeply rutted mud in winter and dust tracks in summer. Only heavy wheeled wagons could tackle these conditions and more often, transport was confined to packhorse trains.

During the seventeenth century regions began to specialize in particular goods. The demand for coal, bricks, building materials and lime (used as a fertilizer) increased the pressure to develop internal trade. The easiest form of transport was the sea passage around Britain and east-coast ports, such as Newcastle and Hull, developed to meet this need. Trading inland presented more difficulties because of poor roads. There were many attempts to improve and increase travel by river and by the 1730s there were 1,850 km of navigable waterways.

Everything this man is wearing was made in different parts of Britain. The information is based on Daniel Defoe's description in his Complete English Tradesman, *1726.*

A pack-horse train carrying goods. This was often the only way that heavy goods could be transported around the country.

The first half of the eighteenth century also saw some improvements in roads. Each parish was supposed to keep its roads in good repair, but they were often neglected or poorly repaired. In 1663 the government permitted a group of businessmen to take over the running of part of the Great North Road (from London to York) and to charge a toll. They were allowed to place a gate, or turnpike, at the entrance to the section of road that they were responsible for. By 1750 there were 143 turnpike trusts (groups), responsible for 5,449 km of road, mainly in and around London and the Midlands. In some instances better roads were constructed. Improvements to road and river travel helped to make the delivery of goods speedier and, in some cases, cheaper.

By the mid-eighteenth century Britain was the most powerful trading nation in the world and poised on the brink of becoming the first industrial nation.

Time Line

1500–1550

◊ **1485** Henry Tudor defeats Richard II at the Battle of Bosworth and becomes Henry VII of England

◊ **1509** Henry VIII becomes king

◊ **1513** The English beat the Scots at the Battle of Flodden

◊ **1534** Henry VIII breaks away from the Church of Rome and becomes head of the Church of England

◊ **1536–9** Dissolution of monasteries

◊ **1547** Edward VI rules England; during his reign England becomes a Protestant country

| 1500 | 1510 | 1520 | 1530 | 1540 | 1550 |

1550–1600

◊ **1553** Mary Tudor succeeds to the throne.

Willoughby and Chancellor attempt North East Passage to India

◊ **1558** Elizabeth I succeeds to the throne

◊ **1560** Introduction of the Poor Law

◊ **1562** Trade in West African slaves begins

◊ **1563** Statute of Apprentices introduced

◊ **1570** Drake's first voyage to West Indies

◊ **1576** Houses of Correction introduced.

Frobisher and Hawkins attempt North West Passage

◊ **1579** Rebellion in Ireland

◊ **1577–81** Drake's circumnavigation of the world

◊ **1585** Drake sent to plunder Spanish ships in West Indies

◊ **1586** Tobacco first introduced into England

◊ **1592** Shakespeare's plays first performed

◊ **1597** Provision of poor relief; first work-houses built

| 1550 | 1560 | 1570 | 1580 | 1590 | 1600 |

1600–1650

◊ **1600** East India Co. set up to trade in the Far East

◊ **1601** Poor Law Act

◊ **1603** James VI of Scotland becomes James I of England

◊ **1607** American colony of Virginia set up

◊ **1611** Authorized Version of the Bible published

◊ **1620** Voyage of Pilgrim Fathers to America.

First Turnpike Act (to improve roads)

◊ **1625** Charles I succeeds to the throne

◊ **1635** First Inland Postal Service set up, between Edinburgh and London

◊ **1642–6** English Civil War between King and Parliament

◊ **1649** Execution of Charles I.

Cromwell invades Ireland.

Introduction of tea into England

| 1600 | 1610 | 1620 | 1630 | 1640 | 1650 |

1650–1700

◊ **1653** Cromwell appointed Lord Protector

◊ **1660** Charles II restored to the throne

◊ **1665** Great Plague at its height in England

◊ **1666** Fire of London

◊ **1685** Accession of James II

◊ **1688** William of Orange invited to restore liberties of England; flight of James II

◊ **1689** William and Mary become King and Queen

◊ **1695** Bank of England established

| 1650 | 1660 | 1670 | 1680 | 1690 | 1700 |

1700–1750

◊ **1701** Invention of horse-drawn drill for planting seeds in rows

◊ **1702** Accession of Queen Anne

◊ **1714** Accession of George I

◊ **1715** Jacobite rebellion in the North defeated

◊ **1722** Workhouse Act

◊ **1724** Fondness for gin drinking develops in England

◊ **1727** George II succeeds to the throne

◊ **1739** Society of Methodists develops

◊ **1741** Highway Act

◊ **1743** Yarns imported into Lancashire from East India

◊ **1745–6** Jacobites rebel in Scotland, defeated at Battle of Culloden

| 1700 | 1710 | 1720 | 1730 | 1740 | 1750 |

Glossary

Ambassador The representative of a foreign country.

Artificers Skilled craftsmen.

Brigs Small coastal sailing ships.

Buccaneer A pirate, especially one who attacked Spanish shipping in the West Indies and South America.

Burgesses Townspeople.

Charity The giving of money, food, shelter etc. to people in need.

Circumnavigate To sail around the world.

Civil war War between people living in the same country.

Colonies Overseas lands where people have settled and are governed by the mother country.

Colonists People who move to settle in another country.

Corn dolly A model or figure made from plaited straw.

Economy The trade and industry of a country.

Empire A group of countries or states governed by one ruler.

Fallow Ploughed land that is left uncultivated for a period.

Fertility Growth or fruitfulness.

Guild An association or group of workers or craftspeople of a particular trade, formed to give each other support and protection and to protect standards.

Husbandman The owner of a small farm.

Journeymen Craftsmen who were employed by different masters (employers).

Malnutrition A poor diet.

Manufactured goods Articles made in a factory or workshop.

Middle Ages The period of British history from 1066 to 1500, sometimes known as the medieval period.

Midwives Women who help a mother during the birth of her baby.

Miracle or mystery plays Religious plays, usually about Bible stories.

Mumming plays Mimes.

Mutilations Injuries resulting in loss of limbs or disfigurement.

Parish A district with its own church and clergyman.

Plague A very serious infectious disease, carried by rats.

Pilgrimage A journey to a holy place.

Plundering Stealing, taking by force, often during wartime.

Propaganda The spreading of ideas or information, often to assist the cause of a government.

Sanitation Arrangements to encourage good health, such as drainage, rubbish disposal and cleanliness.

Squire A country gentleman or landowner.

Stocks A wooden frame for holding a criminal by the ankles or wrists.

Toll A fee charged before vehicles can use certain stretches of road.

Turnpike A gate set across a road to prevent passage until a toll has been paid.

Unhygienic Dirty, unclean conditions.

Vagabond A beggar or thief, usually with no work and no settled home.

Vagrants People with no settled home; another word for tramps.

Yeoman A farmer who owned and worked his own land.

Books to Read

Elizabeth I by Sheila Watson (Wayland, 1995)
Everyday Life in Tudor Times by Haydn Middleton (Simon & Schuster, 1993)
Henry VIII by Katrina Siliprandi (Wayland, 1995)
The Jacobites by Iain Rose (Wayland, 1995)
The Making of the United Kingdom by Peter Hepplewhite and Neil Tonge (Causeway Press, 1992)
Tudor and Stuart Chronicle by J. Mason (Longman, 1993)

For older readers

The English, A Social History by Christopher Hibbert (Harper Collins, 1994)
The Weaker Vessel, Woman's lot in seventeenth-century England by Antonia Fraser (Weidenfeld and Nicolson, 1984)

Places of Interest to Visit

Museum of English Rural Life
The University
Whiteknights
Reading RG6 2AG.
An information centre for the history of the English countryside. Exhibitions include agricultural tools, rural industries and domestic equipment of the period.

National Maritime Museum
Romney Road
Greenwich
London SE10 9NF.
Displays illustrating the role the sea has played in British history.

Scottish Agricultural Museum
Ingliston
Edinburgh, EH2 88NB.
Exhibitions illustrating the history of farming and rural life throughout Scotland.

Weald and Downland Open Air Museum
Singleton
Nr Chichester PO18 0EU.
Original historic buildings which have been rescued and re-erected. These include farm-buildings, Tudor market hall, blacksmith's forge, village school and other buildings of the period.

Welsh Folk Museum
St Fagans
Cardiff CF5 6XB.
Exhibitions illustrating the traditional life and culture of Wales.

York Castle Museum
York YO1 1RY.
Displays include reconstructions of seventeenth and eighteenth century workshops.

Index